Second Edition Printed October 2015

First published in 2015 by Mercer Books

ISBN 978-0-9557127-8-4

Design by Libbla Kelly and
Hannah Condry at Mercer Books
www.mercerbooks.co.uk

WisdomWhileYouWork.com

CONTENTS

WisdomWhileYouWork.com

INTRODUCTION

WISDOM WHILE YOU WORK
An Inspirational Notebook

When I was writing this book the word "understand" was the one that stood out more than any other. Understand yourself; understand others, understand what you are learning. The greatest way to understand is to listen or read - then ask questions and listen again. Never underestimate the power of words. They can make you laugh and cry, inform and empower you, explain to you and shock you. They certainly make the days more interesting!

Communication is the key to life.

SHARE A LINE OF WISDOM WITH A FRIEND
Select a card from the centre pages, tear and share!

We live in a sharing world. Share some wisdom with a friend.
We share everything on the internet, why not see someone face to face
and share with him or her a little note of wisdom.

This book may help you prepare for the road ahead. Life can be complicated, full of responsibility, decisions and concerns. Read these pages, and you may at least be more aware. As life rolls on you will already have some of the tools to deal with it.

Be one step ahead and enjoy using your notebook!

www.WisdomWhileYouWork.com

become WISE
through experiences

I am going to take charge of myself

I am going to make my own decisions when I can.

6
Sums and numbers

HOW vs WHAT

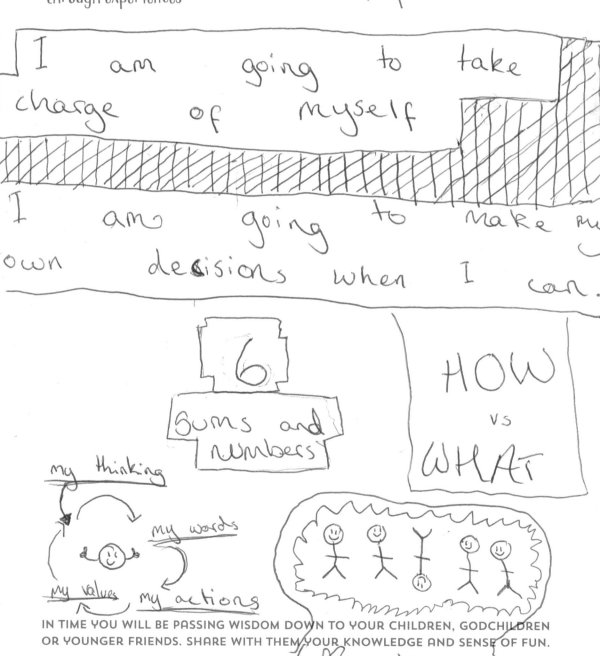

my thinking

my words

my values   my actions

IN TIME YOU WILL BE PASSING WISDOM DOWN TO YOUR CHILDREN, GODCHILDREN OR YOUNGER FRIENDS. SHARE WITH THEM YOUR KNOWLEDGE AND SENSE OF FUN.

diffreat

BE
GENEROUS
WITH COMPLIMENTS

* Lead by EXAMPLE
* Have passion
* Be decisive
* Communicate and Inform
* Be BRAVE, COURAGOUS + DARING
* Dedicated + Listen + Listen + Listen
* take an INTREST
* Delligate
* Flexible and adaptable
* Inspire * Belife
* Energise

BE KIND TO OTHERS, COMMENT ON THEIR CLOTHES OR HAIR,
THIS IS A WIN/WIN SITUATION.
NOT ONLY WILL YOU FEEL KIND, THEY WILL FEEL BETTER ABOUT THEMSELVES.

➤ TIP: BE SINCERE ABOUT THE COMPLIMENTS

read rubbish, listen to rubbish = **SPEAK RUBBISH**

BE **INFORMED**. DON'T WASTE TOO MUCH TIME ON USELESS WEBSITES.
HAVE FUN FOR SURE. REMEMBER - EDUCATE YOUR BRAIN,
LISTEN TO WHAT IS IMPORTANT - FILTER OUT WHAT YOU DON'T NEED.
SPEAK INTELLIGENTLY AND YOUR OPINION WILL BE RESPECTED.

you have
2 EARS AND
1 MOUTH
USE THEM IN PROPORTION

LISTEN... LISTEN... THINK THEN SPEAK.
ENGAGE YOUR BRAIN BEFORE YOU OPEN YOUR MOUTH.
NOTHING WORSE THAN FOOT IN MOUTH!

DON'T
OVER
REACT

ASSESS THE SITUATION QUICKLY AND REASONABLY
- OVER REACTION ALWAYS RESULTS IN APOLOGIES.

IF YOU WANT TO BE GOOD AT SOMETHING,
focus your mind on it

...AGAIN & AGAIN & AGAIN.
IF YOU ACHIEVE SOMETHING, YOU FEEL WONDERFUL.
CONCENTRATE, FOCUS = ACHIEVE

SOMETIMES
YOU HAVE TO DO THINGS

YOU DON'T WANT TO DO

THE SOONER YOU ACCEPT THIS, A BETTER PERSON YOU WILL BE.
PUT UP WITH IT AND GET ON WITH IT. LIFE LESSON - DON'T MOAN.

8

LIFE IS ABOUT WHO YOU ARE WITH
NOT
WHAT YOU HAVE OR CAN BUY

FORGET THE LATEST GADGETS AND WASTING ALL YOUR MONEY ON THEM.
LOOK AT YOUR FRIENDS AND BE THANKFUL FOR THEM.
LAUGHTER, FUN AND MAKING MEMORIES WITH FAMILY AND FRIENDS IS REAL LIFE.

try your
VERY BEST
AND REALLY KNOW
THAT YOU HAVE!

DON'T LIE TO YOURSELF, MAKE SURE YOU HAVE PUT YOUR ALL INTO EVERYTHING
IN LIFE; THE WORST IS TO SAY "I SUPPOSE I COULD HAVE TRIED HARDER."
NO! GO ALL OUT WITH EFFORT AND YOU WILL REAP THE REWARDS.

TAKING SHORT CUTS
CAN BE A RISKY BUSINESS
ON THE ROAD OR IN LIFE!

SHORT CUTS ARE RISKY. ASSESS YOUR RISK FIRST.
IT MAY WORK, BUT HOW SILLY YOU WOULD LOOK IF IT DOESN'T.
THE LONG WAY ROUND MIGHT BE TIME CONSUMING BUT YOU
MAY BE GLAD THAT YOU CHOSE THAT ROUTE.

EAT WELL | FEEL WELL

BEWARE OF PROCESSED FOODS.
TRY AND RESIST SUGAR AND SALT. EAT FRESH VEGETABLES, FRUIT,
FISH OR LEAN MEAT. THE NEARER TO NATURE THE BETTER.

RESPECT
OLDER PEOPLES' IDEAS

THEY HAVE LIVED LONGER, THEREFORE ARE WISER THAN YOU.
TALK TO THEM AND LISTEN TO THEM. BE KIND TO THEM.
ASK THEM QUESTIONS. YOU WILL LEARN SOMETHING. THEY WERE YOUNG ONCE.

USE
YOUR BRAIN
USE IT OR LOSE IT!

LIFE IS ABOUT YOUR BRAIN AND HOW YOU USE IT.
THE LESS YOU USE YOUR BRAIN THE MORE IT WILL FADE!
USE IT, CHALLENGE IT AND LEARN SOMETHING NEW EVERYDAY.
YOUR BRAIN IS YOUR MOST POWERFUL RESOURCE.

IN THE MORNING THINK...

TRY TO BE A GOOD PERSON.
BE KIND, HELPFUL, HAPPY AND ENTHUSIASTIC. SAY "THANK YOU"!

REFLECT ON YOUR DAY. WAS IT A GOOD ONE?
HOW COULD YOU HAVE MADE IT BETTER? TRY HARDER TOMORROW.
NOW SLEEP AND RECHARGE YOUR BATTERIES.

if you are very busy, make sure you are busy at
WORTHWHILE
tasks

IT IS EASY TO BE BUSY DOING NOTHING. TRY AND GENERATE POSITIVE OUTPUT EVERYDAY. DON'T DREAM AWAY THE DAYS, THOSE MINUTES ARE LOST FOREVER.

BE INTERESTED...

...IN WHAT YOU ARE LEARNING.
IF IT IS SCHOOL, COLLEGE, WORK, A COURSE OR JUST LISTENING
TO A WISE PERSON. NEVER STOP LEARNING. NEVER, EVER, EVER!

FIND A HOBBY/INTEREST/PASTIME THAT YOU
L♥VE

IT IS GOOD TO HAVE AN INTEREST - SOMETHING ELSE TO ADD TO YOUR LIST
OF ATTRIBUTES. YOU DON'T HAVE TO BE BRILLIANT AT IT BUT YOU NEED TO ENJOY IT.
A MIXTURE OF WORK HARD, PLAY HARD AND EAT WELL IS A HEALTHY ONE.

ASK QUESTIONS

NOTHING IS MORE CHARMING THAN A POLITE, INTERESTED YOUNG PERSON.
IT SPEAKS VOLUMES. ASK RELEVANT QUESTIONS AND LISTEN TO THE ANSWERS.

don't be frightened of **CHANGE**

CHANGE HAPPENS IN ALL OF OUR LIVES. DON'T FEAR IT. TRY TO EMBRACE IT.
SOMETIMES THINGS ARE BETTER BECAUSE OF CHANGE.
ACCEPT THE THINGS YOU CANNOT CHANGE, CHANGE THE THINGS YOU CAN.
THE BEST THING IS HAVING THE WISDOM TO KNOW THE DIFFERENCE.

LEARN HOW TO CHALLENGE
OR QUESTION skillfully

BE CALM AND RESPECTFUL IN DEBATE, KEEP YOUR HEAD.
UNDERSTAND THAT OTHERS DO BELIEVE THE ABSOLUTE OPPOSITE
TO YOU THOUGH YOU SIMPLY CAN'T BELIEVE IT!

CREATE HARMONY ALL AROUND YOU

LIVING WITH DAILY CONFLICT CAN BE CORROSIVE AND WEARING. DON'T JUST
STAND BACK AND SEE WHAT WILL HAPPEN, SMOOTH OUT THE ROUGH BITS!

BE CAREFUL HOW YOU SPEAK TO
EVERYBODY

NOTHING IS MORE HARSH ON THE EARS THAN BACK CHAT AND RUDENESS,
BREATHE AND THINK BEFORE YOU SPEAK.
OR
PLEASE HELP ME TO KEEP MY BIG MOUTH SHUT UNTIL I KNOW WHAT I AM SAYING.

MAKE THINGS HAPPEN

WAITING FOR THE LIGHT AT THE END OF THE TUNNEL?
YOU HAVE TO GO AND FIND IT. SPARK THE FLAME YOURSELF.

fear
MUST
NOT
CONTROL
YOU

IN ANYTHING YOU DO.
YOU MUST NOT GIVE INTO FEAR. KEEP CALM, BREATHE DEEPLY,
THINK CLEARLY AND FEAR WILL BECOME A THING OF THE PAST.

learn how to
HANDLE
CONFLICT

DON'T GET INVOLVED IN OTHER PEOPLE'S CONFLICTS UNLESS THEY ASK YOU TO.
PERHAPS POLITELY OFFER YOUR HELP. ASK A WISER PERSON OR READ ABOUT
HOW TO DEAL WITH CONFLICT. IT IS HELPFUL TO LEARN THIS SKILL.

ALWAYS BE OPEN

TO OTHER'S POINTS OF VIEW *or* SUGGESTIONS

EVEN IF YOU MAY NOT AGREE WITH THE OTHER PARTY, LISTENING TO
ALL POINTS OF VIEW MAY BROADEN YOUR MIND. THIS IS A GOOD THING.

LOOK AFTER THOSE YOUNGER THAN YOURSELF

TRY TO ENCOURAGE THE RIGHT BEHAVIOUR IN YOUNGSTERS.
THEY LIKE A GOOD MENTOR TO LOOK UP TO, NOT ALWAYS A PARENT OR TEACHER.

learn how to influence in a POSITIVE way

TRY NOT TO SAY 'NO' SAY 'MAYBE'. NEGATIVE ENERGY IS TIRESOME.
BELIEVE IN THE POWER OF POSITIVE THINKING. USE IT TO HELP OTHERS.

ONE OF THE BEST LESSONS IN LIFE IS ONE OF THE OLDEST SAYINGS:

MORE HASTE,

LESS SPEED. THINK ABOUT IT.

always
BEHAVE
WELL

CONTROL
YOURSELF

YOU WILL BE GLAD ABOUT THAT TOO!

KEEP HEALTH (AND) EXERCISE IN YOUR DAILY LIFE

DRINK LOTS OF WATER. EXERCISE DAILY.
REPLACE THE NAUGHTY TAKEAWAYS WITH MORE HOME COOKED FOOD.

NEVER ASK
"HOW ARE YOU?"
AND NOT LISTEN TO THE ANSWER

BE CONCERNED AND SHOW AN INTEREST. TRY AND REMEMBER WHAT THAT
PERSON WAS UP TO THE LAST TIME YOU SAW THEM AND FOLLOW UP ON IT.

DON'T EVER BE STUPID ENOUGH TO THINK YOU KNOW EVERYTHING

NO ONE KNOWS EVERYTHING, WE ARE ALL LEARNING, ALWAYS.
EVERYDAY, TRY AND LEARN SOMETHING NEW AND USEFUL TO
ENHANCE YOUR LIFE AND TO HELP THOSE AROUND YOU.

EMBRACE

WITH AGE COMES RESPONSIBILITY AND YOU HAVE TO ACCEPT YOUR
RESPONSIBILITIES. THINK VERY CAREFULLY BEFORE ACTING ON SOMETHING
THAT MAY CHANGE YOUR LIFE. YOU CANNOT SHIRK RESPONSIBILITY.

AVOID DRINKING TOO MUCH AND MAKING A FOOL OF YOURSELF

RESPECT ALCOHOL. DON'T LET IT BECOME A HABIT. BE IN CONTROL OF IT.

learn the meaning of WORDS

IF YOU DON'T KNOW THE MEANING OF A WORD THEN LOOK
IT UP AND LEARN IT. USE IT TO EXPAND YOUR VOCABULARY.

40

YOU **CAN** BE A
GREAT
SUCCESS

YOU CAN BE ANYTHING YOU WANT TO BE.
HAVE **COURAGE** AND BELIEVE IN YOURSELF.

CARE **ABOUT YOUR APPEARANCE**

CLOTHING, SHOES AND ALL YOU WEAR, MAKE A GOOD FIRST IMPRESSION.
A LITTLE VANITY AND SOME WILLPOWER GOES A LONG WAY.
THINK SMART, BE SMART.

don't bow to peer pressure – it shows weakness

IF YOU KNOW IT'S WRONG DON'T DO IT. MAKE YOUR OWN MIND UP
AND BE BRAVE IF YOU WANT TO DO THE OPPOSITE TO THE CROWD.
BE STRONG AND BE YOUR OWN PERSON.

THINK ABOUT
WHO and WHAT
YOU WANT TO BE

FORM YOUR OWN CHARACTER. WHAT ARE YOU?
LEADER? FOLLOWER? MUSICAL? SPORTY? ACADEMIC? ALL ROUNDER?
FORM YOURSELF.
AVOID THE BAD THINGS IN LIFE AND THE BADDIES WHO TRY AND ENTICE YOU!

DON'T HURT PEOPLE ALONG THE WAY
UNNECESSARILY

WHILE PLOUGHING YOUR OWN FURROW IN LIFE, TRY TO THINK
KINDLY OF OTHERS. DON'T LEAVE SORROW IN YOUR WAKE.

learn how to
ACCEPT
CRITICISM

SHOUTING, SULKING, SHRUGGING, BLUBBERING...NO!
UNDERSTAND WHY YOU ARE BEING CRITICISED.
IF YOU DON'T AGREE, DISCUSS AND DESCRIBE HOW YOU FEEL.
A CONVERSATION IS BETTER THAN A SHOUTING MATCH.

YOU NEED TO BE AWARE OF WHAT
THE SMALL PRINT
MEANS

TAX, INSURANCE, LAWS, TERMS AND CONDITIONS. DON'T BE CAUGHT OUT
BECAUSE YOU "HOPED" IT WOULD BE OK. READ THE DETAILS.

OWN UP ALWAYS AND APOLOGISE IF YOU ARE WRONG

BE BIG ENOUGH TO OWN UP TO YOUR MISTAKES. APOLOGISE AND SUFFER THE CONSEQUENCES OF YOUR ACTIONS. MEAN IT WHEN YOU SAY SORRY.

BE CAREFUL WHA

T YOU WISH FOR...

.....IT MAY COME TRUE.

WHATEVER
YOU ARE DOING
PLAN&
PREPARE

WINGING IT CAN BE A DISASTER. IT IS BETTER TO PREPARE.
FAILING TO PREPARE IS PREPARING TO FAIL.

HAVING
SOMEONE TO
LOVE
IS A
WONDERFUL
THING

RELATIONSHIPS ARE LIKE PLANTS - THEY GROW!
IF YOU LEAVE THEM THEY WILL WITHER AND DIE BUT IF YOU
NURTURE AND FEED AND TEND TO THEM, THEY WILL BLOSSOM!
IF THEY AREN'T WORKING, BE BRAVE ENOUGH TO DEAL WITH IT.

SHOW GRATITUDE

simple gestures make feel-good days!

SAY "THANK YOU" WITH MEANING AND IN A HEARTFELT WAY,
IT CREATES POSITIVE FEELINGS FOR A) THE PERSON YOU THANKED AND B) YOU!

BE TRUE TO YOURSELF

MONEY IS HARD TO SAVE *and* EASY TO SPEND

DON'T OVER REACT

WHATEVER YOU ARE DOING **PLAN & PREPARE**

try your **VERY BEST**  AND **REALLY KNOW THAT YOU HAVE!**

don't be frightened of **CHANGE**

ALWAYS ASK **"WHY?"** IF YOU DON'T UNDERSTAND

SHARE YOUR WORRIES OR CONCERNS

BE INTERESTED...

LEAVE A LASTING IMPRESSION

WisdomWhileYouWork.com

WisdomWhileYouWork.com

WisdomWhileYouWork.com

WisdomWhileYouWork.com

WisdomWhileYouWork.com

WisdomWhileYouWork.com

WisdomWhileYouWork.com

WisdomWhileYouWork.com

WisdomWhileYouWork.com

WisdomWhileYouWork.com

EMBRACE
BEING YOUNG -
BEING OLDER IS HARDER

OWN UP ALWAYS
AND APOLOGISE
IF YOU ARE WRONG

YOU CAN BE A
GREAT
SUCCESS

DON'T HURT PEOPLE ALONG THE WAY
UNNECESSARILY

THINK ABOUT
WHO  and WHAT
YOU WANT TO BE

Listen, then think, then speak

IF YOU
CAN'T DECIDE
- SLEEP ON IT!

HAVE THE
RIGHT
PEOPLE IN
YOUR LIFE

you have

2 EARS AND
1 MOUTH
USE THEM IN PROPORTION

RESPECT
OLDER PEOPLES' IDEAS

WisdomWhileYouWork.com

WisdomWhileYouWork.com

WisdomWhileYouWork.com

WisdomWhileYouWork.com

WisdomWhileYouWork.com

WisdomWhileYouWork.com

WisdomWhileYouWork.com

WisdomWhileYouWork.com

WisdomWhileYouWork.com

WisdomWhileYouWork.com

VALUES, PRINCIPLES AND MORAL COURAGE

KNOW WHAT YOU BELIEVE IN AND STAND BY THOSE BELIEFS.
UNDERSTAND OTHERS' POINTS OF VIEW BUT BELIEVE IN YOURS.

THERE ARE
2 SIDES
TO EVERY STORY

...SOMETIMES MORE

LISTEN TO THE FACTS. SOMETIMES IT'S NOT JUST BLACK AND WHITE.
THERE IS MIDDLE GROUND.
YOU CAN SIT ON THE FENCE OR DECIDE WHICH STAND TO TAKE.

IF YOU CAN'T DECIDE
- SLEEP ON IT!

SOMETIMES LEAVING TIME TO PONDER THINGS BRINGS YOU THE RESULT
YOU ARE LOOKING FOR. TIME CAN PLAY A DECIDING FACTOR. HOWEVER,
IF YOU NEED TO MAKE A QUICK DECISION, REMEMBER WEIGH UP ALL SIDES.

always try to be
CALM, MEASURED AND RATIONAL
in all that you do

KEEPING YOUR COOL CAN BE VERY DIFFICULT.
BUT IT IS A SKILL THAT YOU WILL DEFINITELY BE ADMIRED FOR.

IT HELPS IF YOU KNOW A BIT ABOUT...

...HISTORY, DATES THAT SHAPED OUR COUNTRY, POLITICS, OTHER COUNTRIES, RELIGIONS, CULTURES, THE ECONOMY, WHY WE PAY TAXES, WHAT THEY PAY FOR.

BREATHE!

TAKE DEEP BREATHS WHEN YOU FEEL LIKE YOU ARE LOSING IT.
BREATH GIVES YOU LIFE. WHATEVER YOU ARE DOING
- EXERCISING, SITTING, WALKING OR LYING DOWN -
THINK ABOUT YOUR BREATHING. LEARN ABOUT HOW TO BREATHE CORRECTLY.

know how to quickly
ADD,
SUBTRACT,
MULTIPLY
& DIVIDE...

... AND HOW TO DO PERCENTAGES - YOU WILL NEED MATHEMATICS
EVERY DAY OF YOUR LIFE - LIKE IT OR NOT, IT'S BEST TO LEARN IT.

"ALWAYS ASK WHY?" IF YOU DON'T UNDERSTAND

DON'T WORRY IF YOU FEEL FOOLISH. IT DOESN'T MATTER.
IT IS BETTER TO HAVE THE CORRECT INFORMATION THAN PRETEND
TO KNOW AND LOOK LIKE A FOOL LATER.

KEEP
FIT
IN SOME WAY

YOU MUST TRY AND RAISE YOUR HEARTBEAT EVERYDAY EVEN IF YOU ONLY HAVE
TIME TO WALK FAST. YOUR HEART IS A MUSCLE THAT NEEDS TO BE EXCERCISED.

HAVE THE RIGHT PEOPLE IN YOUR LIFE

CHOOSE YOUR FRIENDS CAREFULLY.
TRY AND SPEND QUALITY TIME WITH THOSE YOU TRULY WANT TO BE WITH.

IT IS NEVER TOO EARLY TO SAVE MONEY.
LEARN ABOUT MONEY, UNDERSTAND FINANCE AND HOW MONEY CAN HELP YOU.
RESPECT MONEY AND NEVER LET GREED GET THE BETTER OF YOU!

TIME FLIES

OLD AGE CREEPS UP MUCH FASTER THAN YOU THINK!
LIVE FOR THE DAY. LAUGH EVERYDAY.

try to have
5 minutes of
SILENCE
every day

JUST EMPTY YOUR MIND, PEACE AND QUIET MAY GIVE CLARITY AND STRENGTH.

TRY TO
UNDERSTAND
POLITICS
BE INTERESTED IN YOUR COUNTRY & HOW IT IS RUN

UNDERSTAND WHAT POLITICAL PARTIES STAND FOR AND WHAT THEIR
IDEOLOGIES ARE. TRY AND BE CLEAR ABOUT YOUR CHOICE OF PARTY.

UNDERSTAND THE WORLD'S RELIGIONS & THEIR BELIEFS

SOME SAY THE WORLD IS RUN BY MONEY AND RELIGION AND
WHO HAS THE MOST OIL. LEARN WHY THESE ARE IMPORTANT.

BLAMING OTHERS IS NOT
A GOOD CHARACTER TRAIT

TREAD CAREFULLY; MAKE SURE YOU HAVE THE FACTS STRAIGHT BEFORE
YOU GO POINTING FINGERS AT PEOPLE, IF YOU HAVE TO POINT AT ALL.

learn a
POEM,
SAYING
OR SONG
to amuse people

YOU NEVER KNOW WHEN YOU NEED TO STAND ON A TABLE AND SAY OR SING IT WITH STYLE!

LEAVE A LASTING IMPRESSION

LEAVE A MEMORY OF WARMTH TO THOSE YOU MEET FOR THE FIRST TIME.
MAKE THEM FEEL THEY WOULD BE PLEASED TO SEE YOU AGAIN.

DO NOT LET OUR
GREAT
ENGLISH LANGUAGE
SLIP AWAY

USE IT PROPERLY. SPELL WORDS CORRECTLY, DON'T SHORTEN EVERYTHING.
LEARN GRAMMAR E.G. WHEN TO USE I AND ME CORRECTLY!
IT SOUNDS OLD FASHIONED BUT BELIEVE ME (NOT I!) IT IS VERY IMPORTANT.
WHEN YOU ARE OLDER YOU WILL AGREE!

LAUGH, LAUGH, LAUGH

and make others laugh

DON'T GET SO BOGGED DOWN THAT YOU LOSE YOUR
SENSE OF HUMOUR. SHARE YOUR LAUGHTER WITH OTHERS.

cherish
your friends

KNOW THEIR IMPORTANCE IN YOUR LIFE.
MAKE AN EFFORT TO KEEP IN TOUCH. YOUR FRIENDS ARE PRICELESS.

MAKE
MEMORIES
REMEMBER THEM AND SMILE

IF YOU CAN SEE, SMELL AND HEAR, MAKE MEMORIES WITH ALL OF YOUR SENSES.
WHEN YOU THINK BACK THEY MAKE YOU SMILE AND FEEL WARM INSIDE.

SHARE
YOUR WORRIES OR CONCERNS

WHATEVER YOUR WORRIES OR CONCERNS, BIG OR SMALL, SHARE THEM
WITH SOMEONE. PREFERABLY TELL A WISE PERSON WHO CAN HELP YOU.
DON'T BOTTLE THINGS UP, THEY WILL EAT AWAY INSIDE YOU.

LOOK AFTER EACH OTHER
– WHOEVER YOU ARE CLOSE TO

CARE FOR THEM. LOVE IS PRECIOUS, IT CAN BRING SADNESS TOO, BUT IT
IS BETTER TO HAVE LOVED AND LOST THAN NEVER TO HAVE LOVED AT ALL.

TRUST

IS ONE OF THE MOST IMPORTANT VALUES

DON'T WASTE YOUR TIME WITH SOMEONE YOU CAN'T TRUST. THEY WILL
ALWAYS LET YOU DOWN. LISTEN TO YOUR DOUBTS AND ADDRESS THEM.

YOU WILL LEARN THAT SOMETIMES
LIFE ISN'T FAIR

SOMETIMES THERE IS NOTHING YOU CAN DO TO SAVE A SITUATION.
ACCEPT THIS AND TAKE A POSITIVE FROM IT.

YOU
CANNOT
WIN EVERY ARGUMENT

YOU ARE NOT ALWAYS RIGHT!
LEARN ONE OF LIFE'S GREATEST LESSONS, YOU MAY HAVE TO AGREE TO DISAGREE.

UNDERSTAND LOYALTY

BE LOYAL AND BE A LOYAL FRIEND

LOY·AL·TY

NOUN

1. A FEELING OR ATTITUDE OF DEVOTED ATTACHMENT OR AFFECTION
2. FAITHFUL

HOW WONDERFUL IS THAT?

ALWAYS **WRITE** THANK YOU LETTERS

PREFERABLY BY POST IN YOUR HANDWRITING. THEY MEAN SO MUCH MORE
THAN AN EMAIL - SOME THINGS MUST NEVER CHANGE.

KNOW YOUR
HISTORY

OUR HERITAGE IS VERY IMPORTANT

TRY AND LEARN THE BASIC HISTORY OF THE WORLD WE LIVE IN.
BE ESPECIALLY KNOWLEDGABLE ABOUT YOUR OWN COUNTRY.

DON'T DON'T DON'T
LIE, LIE, LIE.

IT JUST MAKES LIFE SO COMPLICATED.
ONCE YOU LIE YOU WILL FIND IT CREATES A WEB OF LIES AND
YOU WILL WISH YOU HAD TOLD THE TRUTH IN THE BEGINNING.

FEEL HAPPY

EVERYDAY...

TRY AND LIVE WITH HAPPINESS IN SOME FORM EVERY DAY.
SMILING IS GOOD FOR YOU. SMILE IN THE MIRROR IN THE MORNING.
FILL OTHERS' LIVES WITH HAPPINESS TOO.

get things
DONE

DON'T JUST THINK ABOUT THEM

MAKE LISTS AND TICK THEM OFF AS YOU GO. THERE ARE FEW THINGS
MORE SATISFYING THAN A FINISHED LIST! AFTER THAT YOU CAN DAYDREAM!

HAVING FAITH
ISN'T JUST A RELIGIOUS THING

IT MEANS TRULY BELIEVING AND HAVING TRUST
AND CONFIDENCE IN SOMETHING OR SOMEONE.

...To engage a situation

a storise to illastrate
   a point

word s that are
       b . intuchable
inperitive

        P you   us   we

☐ POVERTY
☐ CAPITALISM
☐ SOCIALISM
☐ RACISM
☐ WAR
☐ MONEY
☐ RELIGION
☐ ART

JUST IN CASE YOU ARE STUCK FOR A TOPIC!

life is too short

HOW SHORT? SOMETIMES LIFE CAN FEEL LONG AND DIFFICULT AND PAINFUL.
MAKE THE BEST OF IT AND TRY TO JUST LIVE FOR THE DAY YOU ARE LIVING IN.

every day
SPARE A THOUGHT FOR THOSE LESS FORTUNATE THAN YOURSELF

−T + D

2

U

−S +TH

−T +W

−B + G

1:2   HORSEMEAT
3:2   DRESS TO KILL

U

−N +TH

?

THERE IS MUCH SADNESS IN THE WORLD;
PEOPLE WHO ARE POOR, SAD, LONELY, BEREAVED, DISPLACED.
EVERY DAY SPARE A THOUGHT OR PRAYER FOR THEM.

91

BE HAPPY

IN YOUR OWN COMPANY

IT'S GOOD TO LEARN TO BE ALONE, IT IS SO DIFFERENT FROM BEING LONELY.
SPEND SOME TIME ALONE, GO TO A MUSEUM, GALLERY OR FOR A WALK IN THE
COUNTRYSIDE, PONDER LIFE. CLEAR YOUR HEAD. DO YOUR HOBBY.

LOOK AT YOUR LIFE
as if reading a book

CHAPTERS START AND FINISH, SOME BETTER THAN OTHERS, BUT
TAKE THE CHANCE TO MAKE EACH CHAPTER EVEN BETTER THAN THE LAST.

STAND BY YOUR FRIENDS

YOU DON'T HAVE TO BE INVOLVED IN EVERYTHING THEY DO,
BUT STAND BY THEM IN TIMES OF DIFFICULTY AND SADNESS.

DEAL WITH
THE PROBLEMS YOU HAVE

OTHERWISE THEY WILL JUST COME BACK AND BITE YOUR LAZY BEHIND!

LIVE YOUR LIFE
NOT OTHER PEOPLES'

SHARE YOUR LIFE, YES, BUT IT IS STILL YOUR OWN LIFE AND ALWAYS WILL BE.
ONLY YOU ARE COMPLETELY ON YOUR SIDE ALL YOUR LIFE!
LIVE YOUR LIFE THE BEST WAY YOU POSSIBLY CAN!

STAY HYDRATED = DRINK WATER

REMEMBER TO DRINK WATER, IT'S EASY TO FORGET! KEEP YOUR BODY
FUNCTIONING PROPERLY - BRAIN, HAIR & SKIN THEY ALL NEED HYDRATING.

go with what YOU have got

HOWEVER LITTLE YOU HAVE, IT'S A START. USE IT TO GET YOU GOING.

THINK ABOUT YOUR

POSTURE

EVERY DAY

KEEPING YOUR SHOULDERS BACK, YOUR TUMMY IN, YOUR HEAD UP AND YOUR BACK STRAIGHT CAN HELP YOU TO LOOK TALLER, BE MORE CONFIDENT AND IMPROVE YOUR BREATHING. IT IS SO IMPORTANT TO CARE FOR YOUR SPINAL CORD, IT CARRIES SO MANY IMPORTANT MESSAGES TO THE REST OF YOUR BODY ALL DAY.

REMEMBER THE GREATEST LIFE TIP OF ALL

BE TRUE TO YOURSELF

THIS MEANS KNOWING THAT YOU HAVE DONE THE BEST YOU CAN
EVERY DAY IN THE MOST HONEST, KIND, FRIENDLY, FUN WAY POSSIBLE.

ABOUT THE AUTHOR

Libbla Kelly (nee Pigot) was born in Dublin in 1965. Later the
Pigots moved to Somerset, England where her parents had
originally met. Growing up, the family home was full of fun-loving
people, young and old, a joyful hub of care and communication.
Libbla became a Nanny, and having 12 Godchildren, 4 nieces and
nephews and likened to the Pied Piper, she knew she connected
well with the young. Her career with children, management
training, personal training and working with an entrepreneur for
20 years has culminated in this book. It started off as a letter to
her godchildren and ended up as Wisdom While You Work - An
Inspirational Notebook - a journal of communication - sharing hints
and essential messages about life for young people today.

THANKS TO...

TED MONICA PIPS NICK BIL CAROLYN DAVO MLY
DREW HETTY HIME CHARM MAORI POOH KIRSTY
TITO MONKS EMS ARCHIE POD JAMPS MICKO PEN
JACKIE FRANCIS HUGH JOE GRACEFUL ALICE
ANASTASIA U GEORGE H VAN ZELLER MILLIE
SEAMUS RORY OLIVIA CAMILLA GAV A SUTCH
CHARTS SOIZE SUSLES MEL SIMON HATPIN
WILL EVIE MASH MATILDA GEORGE C CONNIE
ANNABEL TOM HAM DIANE LELLS MIME FREDDIE
MELLOTTES TIM GINA DOWNSIDE OZ MUSIC
FILMS BADGER BETTY GRANNY FITZ O REILLYS
POVE SWEEP EKES COUSINS GILES PIGOTS
IRELAND ORCHARDS HENDOS WALLYS JAMES'S
CAROLINE JENNINGS MILNES RADCLIFFES OUR
LADY LOURDES FRIENDS GYM HARPER LEE
STRATTON BOD BRUCE BONO AND OTHERS NOT
HERE BUT NOT FORGOTTEN!

...LIBBLA